William Tucker

CW01670293

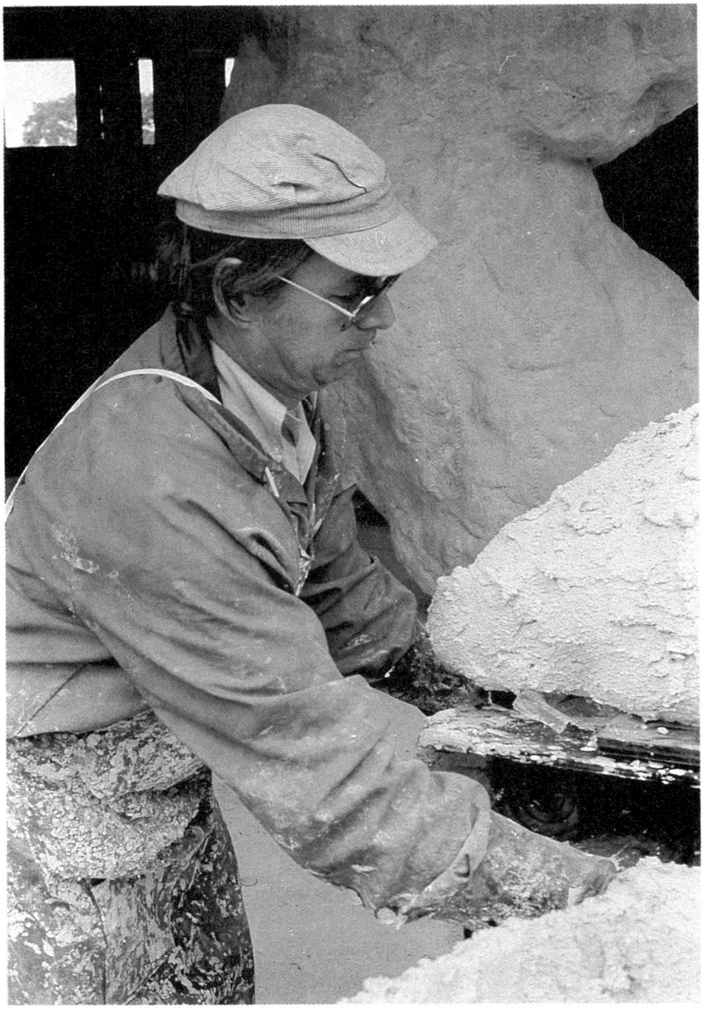

William Tucker

GODS : FIVE RECENT SCULPTURES

The Tate Gallery

cover
Tethys 1986
(plaster for bronze, cat.no.4)

ISBN 0 946590 78 8
Published by order of the Trustees 1987
for the exhibition of 8 July - 23 August 1987
Copyright © 1987 The Tate Gallery All rights reserved
Designed and published by Tate Gallery Publications,
Millbank, London SWIP 4RG
Printed by The Hillingdon Press, Uxbridge, Middlesex

Foreword

William Tucker - sculptor, teacher, exhibition organiser, writer and critic - has not exhibited in London for several years. We are delighted to be able to show in our Gallery of New Art a group of five recent sculptures, entitled Gods, which are the result of a year's intense work.

Tucker now lives mainly in New York. In the 1960s he belonged to the small group of major British sculptors associated with the St Martin's School of Art, where he studied and taught, using such modern materials as painted sheet metals and fibreglass. This work revolutionised our concept of sculpture. Tucker represented Great Britain at the Venice Biennale of 1972, and has exhibited widely in Europe and America. He has also established himself as the most articulate sculptor of his generation, with books and essays that have demonstrated a profound understanding of the art and craft of sculpture, together with a sense of history and his own place in it. It is perhaps in this context that Tucker's remarkable new works should be regarded.

We are most grateful to all those who have helped to realise this exhibition, in particular Carla Panicali of L'Isola Gallery, Rome, and Vanessa Jalet of Art for Architecture, New York. I should particularly like to thank the distinguished American teacher and art critic, Dore Ashton, for her illuminating catalogue essay, and Tom Bendhem for his generous contribution towards the transport costs. Finally, our warmest thanks go to the artist himself, without whose support and cooperation the exhibition would not have been possible.

Alan Bowness *Director*

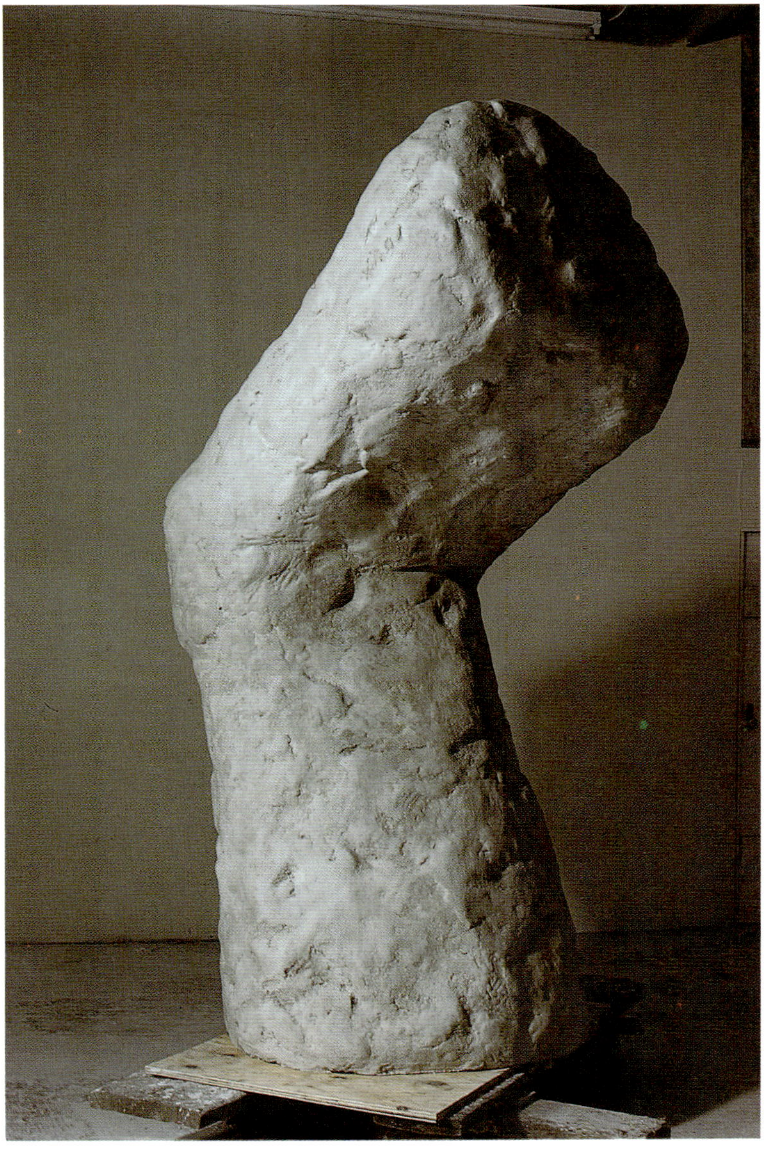

Rhea 1985 (plaster for bronze, cat.no.1)

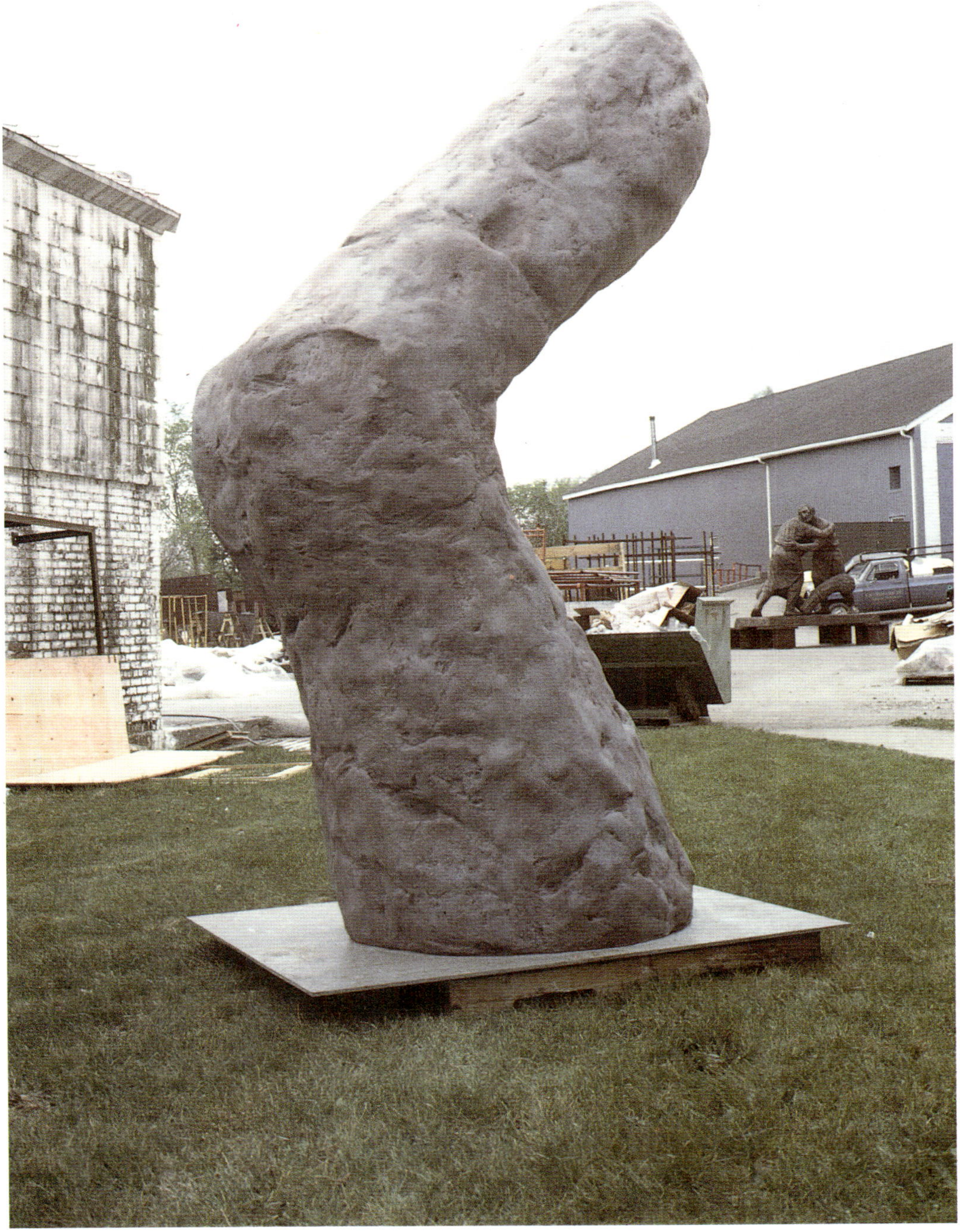

Rhea 1985 (cat.no.1)

William Tucker's Aspiration

Here are five sculptures that retrieve bodily presence from the limbo to which it was consigned early in the century. Performing an emphatic gesture of incarnation, Tucker makes trivial the fine distinctions between mass and volume - all those learned arguments that have done so little to advance our understanding of sculptural space. In the thundering force producing these great hulking lumpish lurching weighty things that inevitably carry the memory of bodies, Tucker springs free. These five sculptures - the fruit of a year's intense dedication - are objects that are somewhere between a human figure and an ancient metaphor; between a downright object and a gesture. They are as shocking, as wildly unlikely in his oeuvre as Rodin's 'Torso of Ugolino' that, as Catherine Lampert has observed, seems rather like a rock or an unearthed remain than a statue.[1] These torsos by Tucker - for basically they are meant to be torsos - are no less rocklike and 'unearthed'. In their ancient titles, in their very shape, they tell of Tucker's will to pull up full-bodied presences from a consecrated clay that offers timeless resistance.

Tucker, whose thoughtful meander through modern sculpture history spans almost twenty-five years, has never flinched from the tasks of an intellectual. He has consistently questioned the history of his art and his own assumptions. He goes where his spirit (rather, *esprit*) prompts. In so doing he risks misunderstanding. An audacious group of works such as these five sculptures with their powers to unnerve and confound inevitably raises questions. Since Tucker had for years built an international reputation on sculpture that effectively shunned mass and the figure, the questions are crucial. (When someone asked deKooning, who had stunned the art world with his 'Woman' series, why he had 'gone back' to the figure, he answered, why not?) The visual intellectual casts out shibboleths.

But not always at the beginning. I'm sure that when Tucker embarked on his early works, such as the bent sheet-metal pieces that move stealthily up from the floor ('Orpheus', for instance), he was quite willing to accept the modernist dictum that less is more. Or the instructions issued like bullets by the constructivists: Do not displace space. Encompass it. Do not fill up your volumes with mass. Make virtual volumes. Tucker's earlier abstract sculptures issued from that tradition, to which he added an acute accent and a singular insight that enabled him eventually to move on. Gabo suggested in the 1920 manifesto that the constructivist vision would wholly eliminate mass in favour of line: 'We

[1] *Rodin Sculpture and Drawings*, Arts Council of Great Britain, 1987

bring back to sculpture the line as a direction and in it we affirm depth as the one form of space'. Tucker's work of the mid to late 1960s certainly depends on line, which he shapes with cunning shifts in perspective to invoke rather complex depths. Virtually. I think of certain of the 'Cat's Cradle' group with their spidery lines opening unexpectedly into ambiguous spaces, in which Tucker creates arcane geometries of his own; establishes a canon for himself that is highly personal. The very title says something about his intellectual and sensory ductility. A cat's cradle, after all, is a figure in space that can only be imagined as a making. Every child has participated at one time or another in the making of it. There is a distinct satisfaction in the shaping of space; of actually holding it in one's hand. Here space is a medium in which shapes are magically evoked. The leading strings do not describe so much as suggest figures. The virtual triumphs.

In the early 1970s Tucker began giving his steel members, now both rectilinear and round in shape, as in the 'Porte' series, a certain heft, increasing the tensions within his open, virtual spaces. At the same time he was clearly questioning himself, as became obvious when he published his book *Early Modern Sculpture* in which he alludes to the peculiar crisis in sculpture, and begins to define the essential nature of sculpture in terms of the convention that acknowledges gravity:[2] 'A sense of gravity, of a strong relation between the form of the object and the ground on which it lies, has been central to the most vital modern sculpture since Rodin. . . A sense of gravity is the factor which mediates our visual perception of sculpture with our conceptual knowledge of its "real" form'. A year later, in his introduction to the Arts Council exhibition *The Condition of Sculpture*, he describes the pressure on modern sculpture to adopt the 'painting-directed role of relief', and expresses some dissatisfaction. (A close reading of that important text indicates the turning in Tucker's way of thinking about his own sculpture.) 'Sculpture is subject to gravity and is revealed by light. Here is the primary condition. Gravity governs sculpture's existence in itself, light discloses sculpture to us.' His 'counter-revolution', as he had called it earlier, begins to take shape when he states: 'When we speak of sculpture as "active" we do so metaphorically: at most it resists our gaze, receives light, withstands gravity'. Here he specifically rejects the constructivist position, and in his final paragraph prophesies his own eventual moves:

> Sculpture's free-standing is thus more than a neutral description: it is an aspiration. To stand free, for sculpture, demands a positive acceptance and understanding of its condition; and it follows that a free sculpture will remain inconvenient, obtrusive – a challenge to facile and conventional views of history and aesthetic.

[2] *Early Modern Sculpture*, N.Y., Oxford, 1974

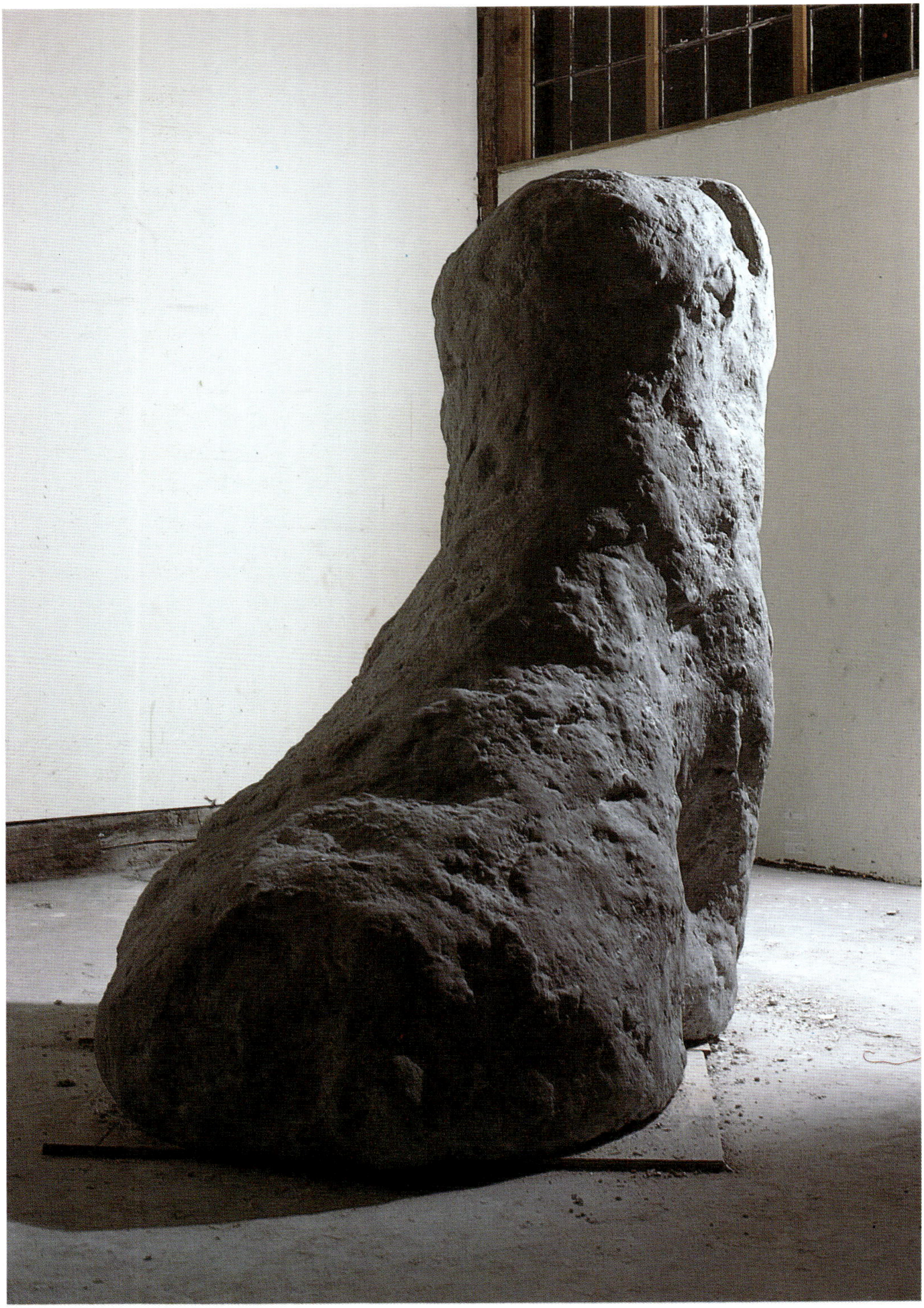

Ouranos 1985 (plaster for bronze, cat. no.2)

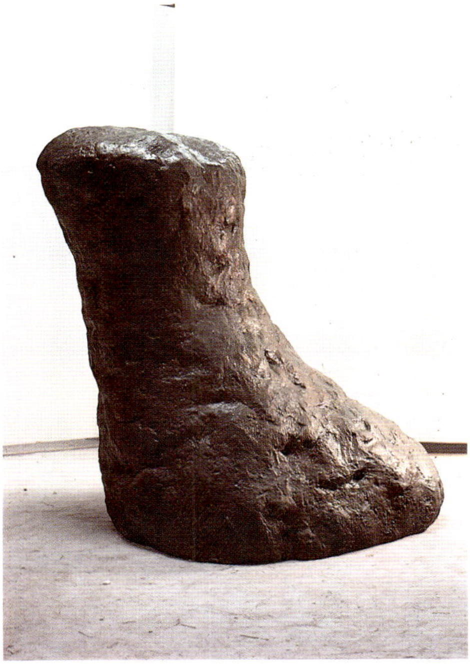

Ouranos 1985 (cat. no.2)

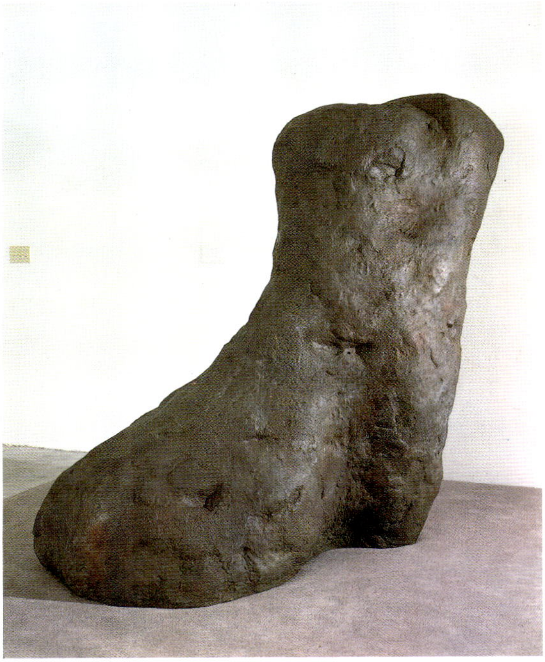

Ouranos 1985 (cat.no.2)

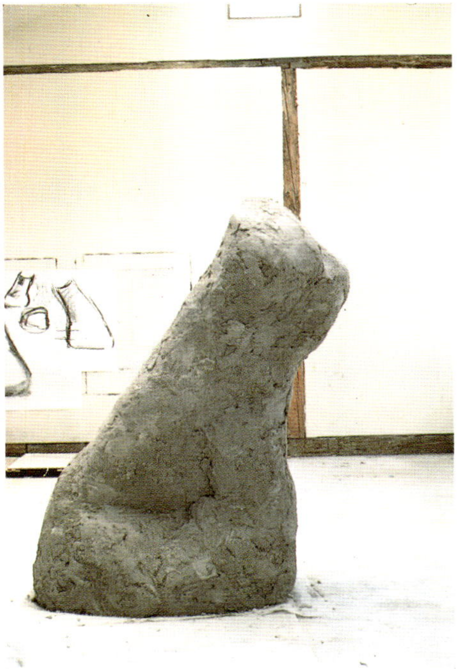

Kronos 1985 (plaster for bronze, cat.no.3)

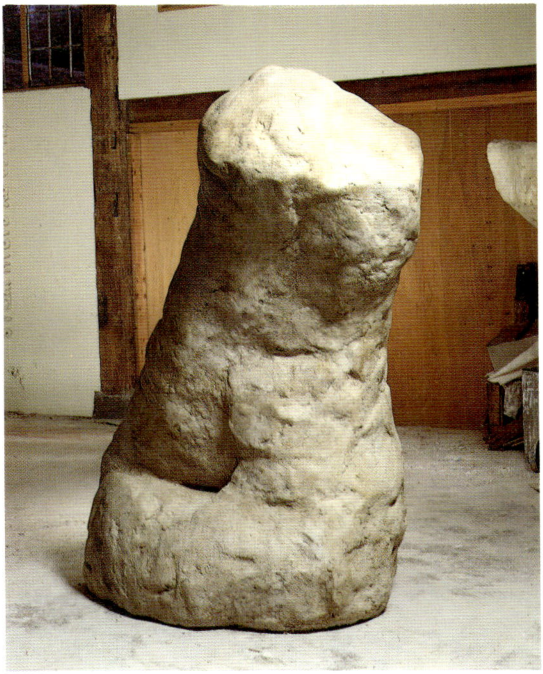

Kronos 1985 (plaster for bronze, cat.no.3)

It was around the time he was organising the large international exhibition for the Arts Council that Tucker was reviewing - literally - his own work, and seeing in it a new potential. His sculptures that had once been almost purely linear, and had adhered to the principle of multiple infinities, now began to suggest interiors and exteriors in clear definition. Using rougher materials such as weathered timbers, he constructed irregular basic shapes - the triangles and pyramids he still utilises as imaginary armatures - that had metaphorical implications of shelter or, in some cases, prisons. The blunt phrasing in these sculptures insisted that the viewer understand their 'free standing' inner nature. The glory of that epoch in Tucker's creative life was probably the huge wood sculpture, later cast in bronze, called 'The Rim', a wheel almost fifteen feet in diameter that in its rhythms, its irregularities, its inexplicably powerful centrifugal motion was the summum of Tucker's meditation on the nature of his art. This was no mere drawing in space, but a real *thing*, an object that stood high and, curiously enough, did not invite the spectator to move through its diaphanous central space, as virtual as it was.

Probably not even the artist himself could explain why, sometime in the early 1980s, he experienced a great hunger for the thinglike mass that the art of the modeller creates. Perhaps it was a simple matter of surfeit. After all, there have been astonishing stylistic shifts in the twentieth century that can only be accounted for as the craving for change that comes after an overabundance of any kind. The century had seen the art of sculpture increasingly condensed until, as Tucker himself showed, it was sometimes the mere wisp of a hairfine line floating into infinity. Now Tucker needed the other experience: he coveted the sense of life that drags itself up, struggles from its stern magnet, the ground, to unknown realms of feeling. He wanted to take a lump of matter and shape it, pull it, so that it rose and stood in the world, a thing. Some of the experiments with plaster in the early 1980s would take on the lineaments of figures struggling into resistant spaces. They sprang forward or back in anthropomorphic gestures. In the 'Guardians' there were distinct allusions to the thrust of bodies; true torsion that might have been mined from the substance of Michelangelo's slaves. The 'Gymnasts' that followed were still more suggestive. Tucker embodied gestures, or rather, made physical metaphors that suggested gestures, while holding the objects to the ground by their enormous implied weight. These pieces lunging into space were scarcely larger than a man, but they had all the implications of massive, even monumental sculpture. They spoke of deep intuitions. Effort. Resisting gravity is no mean feat. They struggled up like Beethoven's Grosse Fugue, that jarring, scraping ascent to the crescendo: lifelikeness. The shock of these lumpy presences and the extremist nature of the analogue to human emotions brought Tucker to the brink of an outright figurative art. But the 'aspiration' of which he had once spoken is larger. Tucker created presences that overwhelmed their designated space; jostled them and shaped them, and gathered up in their being references that range far wider than merely the human figure in his upright contest with the forces of nature.

In order to fully experience the five sculptures with their anhistorical titles and their clear allusion to primordial echoing (as sounds echo in their eternal circuit within an amphora buried after some Odyssean shipwreck), a viewer must seek the interior geometry and feel his way outward. He must, as Tucker has said, feel with his own body, for everything he builds is a relation between the body - his or the spectator's - and the sculpture. In these five sculptures Tucker has taken back mass; has deliberately built dense, heavy objects that in their final profiles are highly ambiguous. All kinds of transformations occur as we walk around these free-standing sculptures, some so minute as to be subliminal, some quite visibly astonishing. Working in that mythic realm fashioned by the ancient Greeks, Tucker has found ways to suggest the constant metamorphoses that occur, the shape-shifting with which the ancient gods played. He has restated old conventions about sculpture (that it must be free-standing in space, or, as they used to say, in-the-round) with such force that he has drawn a new convention from the old. This, very important, mission is implicit. (Even Gabo in later years may have had second thoughts about the tenets of the original manifesto. He concedes that everyone has admired the 'Victory of Samothrace' for its 'so-called dynamic rhythms, the imaginary forward movement incorporated in this sculpture', but points out that the feeling of motion is an illusion and exists only in our minds. 'The real Time does not participate in this emotion; in fact, it is timeless.' Tucker might respond: Precisely!)

The strange thing is that even though it is we who move around these implacably thinglike sculptures, they also move, ponderously but inexorably, and from within. Tucker has not given up the plumb-line reference to the standing human figure. Each of the five sculptures has multiple axes, but one dominant vertical axis, reminding us, as Matisse did in his text for 'Jazz', that man is always the measure. Matisse expressed this ancient sentiment very well and I suspect that Tucker, a deep student of Matisse's sculpture, assimilated the wisdom: 'I have derived constant benefit from my use of the plumb-line', Matisse wrote. 'There is something vertical in my spirit. It helps me give my lines a precise direction . . .' The lines of the five sculptures are never purely descriptive. They are sensed as interiority. Within those almost shapeless curving volumes given by the essential plumb-line there are directions. Tucker is not speaking about space as such, but about substance. Substance within space. Substances that are bodily. (When the ageing Canova finally saw the Elgin marbles he exclaimed: *É carne, vera carne* - it's flesh, real flesh.) These substances form a whole group around a vertical. And they embody movement. They *express* movement, but they are visibly immovable.

The shapes that move out from the impenetrable centre of each of these sculptures hover on the edge of amorphousness. They are nearly, but never absolutely, extinguished by the intuitive hand that gropes its

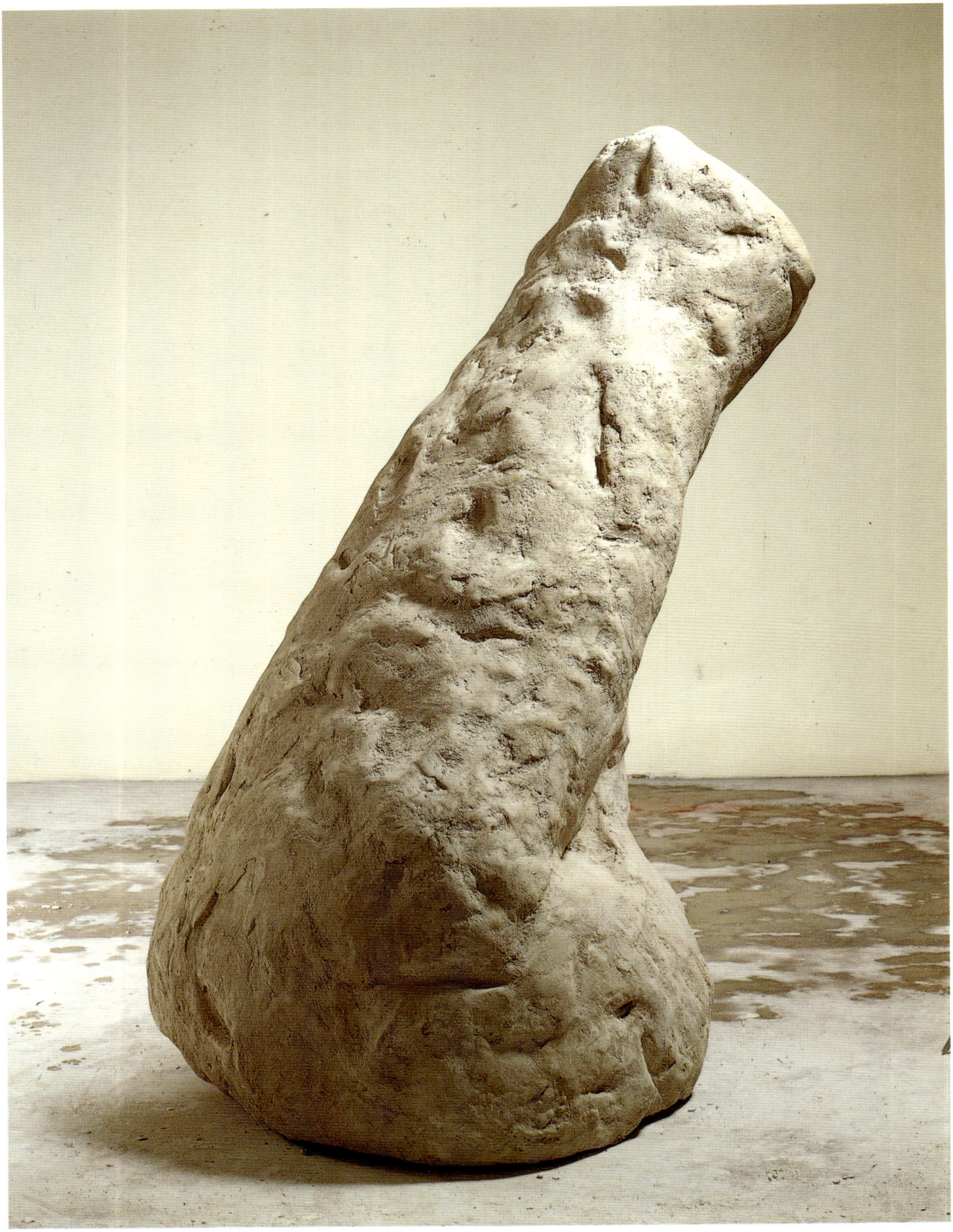

Kronos 1985 (plaster for bronze, cat.no.3)

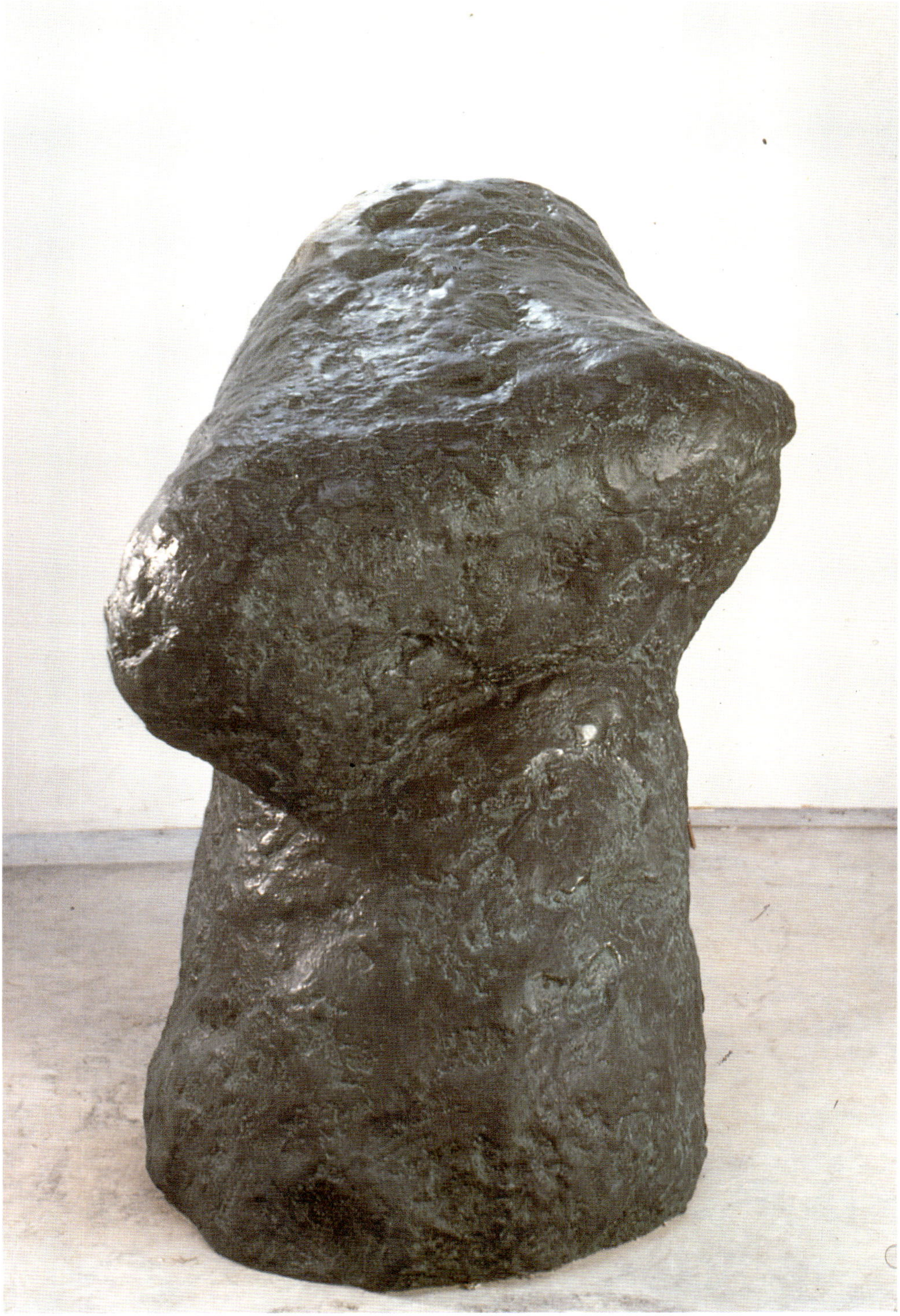

Tethys 1986 (cat.no.4)

way along the large curving surfaces. There is something immensely exciting about this nearly, but not, shapelessness. When Tucker gives a few crucial visual directions, as he does in 'Kronos' where a fold near the base prompts associations with the torsion of flesh, a complex being (or becoming?) is conjured. Still more is this so in 'Tethys', wife of Ocean, where the various axes are quite reasonable and readable, or so it seems at first glance. A vertical, a clear diagonal, and subsidiary repetitions of these basic lines seem to govern the ensemble of forms rather strictly. But the instant the viewer begins his circular inspection, everything changes. The cresting plane on the diagonal now seems boundless. The slope is enormous. One puts one's hand, at shoulder height, to the flank of this solid, vaguely round mass, and it moves into a vastness that is unaccountable. Or perhaps can be accounted for by the erratic transitions from shallow hollow to low boss. Unquestionably, the feeling generated by the swelling shapes derives from some kind of physical response that aestheticians and psychologists have never succeeded in defining.

The disturbing character of this instinctive response can be fully savoured in 'Gaia'. It stands with considerable aplomb in a strangely fashioned void in which gravity openly quarrels with the sculpture's stability. It feels top heavy, yet once we begin our peregrination round its flanks, shapes announce themselves that could not have been 'seen' but only felt at whatever point we begin our circuit. Now it is seen with a strange overhang, casting a shadow, now it is seen as a massive curved back, thrusting into the winds of time. This protean quality in all five sculptures almost certainly derives from Tucker's choice of material and his method of working. He deliberately selected plaster, made somewhat grainy with fragments of a gypsum-like material. Plaster can be modelled, like earth, but it has its term. It must all be done quickly, for there is an implicit absolute there. Plaster sets itself determinedly within some fifteen or twenty minutes. Tucker's decision to work with this malleable but potentially absolute material fortified his will to create solid bodies in space. Moreover, these large sculptures were not planned in drawings. Tucker worked with small models he had created intuitively, swiftly, and with modicum of detail. They could reside in the space of his hand. Out of these quick and intuitive experiences he built up his masses, always allowing himself discoveries en route.

In this, his method has many affinities with the abstract expressionist painters. Guston, for instance, remarked that at a certain point he no longer wished to 'stand back' from his canvas. The intimate, up close experience of the material and its support was important to release impulses that were, in his previous methods of composing, locked up. In fact, it is curious that Tucker's sculpture, with its emphasis on the expressive character of shape that seems to metamorphose and yet is basically a shape, is the first attempt to work with what are companion principles, in sculpture, to abstract expressionism. The sculptors working during the years of the movement were, oddly enough, never aware of the possibilities. Tucker's recent sculptures have more in common with deKooning and Guston than with David Smith. But then, such delays and curiosities are not unusual in the history of art.

What Tucker's sculpture shares with the abstract expressionist vision is the shocking effect of the large body seen close up. Picasso had already determined that a part of a body - a finger joint, elbow or knee - brought up close and distorted in its enlargement, creates disturbing and powerfully expressive aesthetic effects. DeKooning and others in the movement took their cues from Picasso. Now Tucker extends the tradition to the third dimension, complete with substances and shadows. 'Rhea', for instance: it can be seen as an accretion of human associations: it rears up, it turns, at once a knee, a thigh, a back, a figure dipping in a clumsy minuet. The light models cunningly so that the shadowed skin has the roundness of human limbs. Yet when seen frontally (assuming there are four major views here), the sculpture assumes an unnervingly ambiguous shape. We cannot name it. We cannot embrace this trunk with our arms. Yet this thing is very much a presence (an intruder?) in our space. His sculptures in this group of five are *all* perceived as occupying our space. We can bump into them. They hit the floor as we do, and there is a folding-in at their base, a rounding that suggests their status as metaphors for organic beings. But they are also sculptures that defy a single glance and demand close scrutiny. They are at once invaders of our space and space itself, solidified. When seen together - and they are best seen as a troglodytic gathering - they are shockingly present. They bespeak the essential duality in sculpture, as Tucker construes it, between its internal, physical, and its external, perceived nature. The elements - materials, structure, volumes, space - do not function separately but rather, as he said in his book, 'articulate a complex and profound sense of our own being in the world'. Sculpture's condition of free standing, as epitomised in these five works, is certainly more than what Tucker called neutral design; it is, as he said, an aspiration: one that he has fulfilled.

Dore Ashton

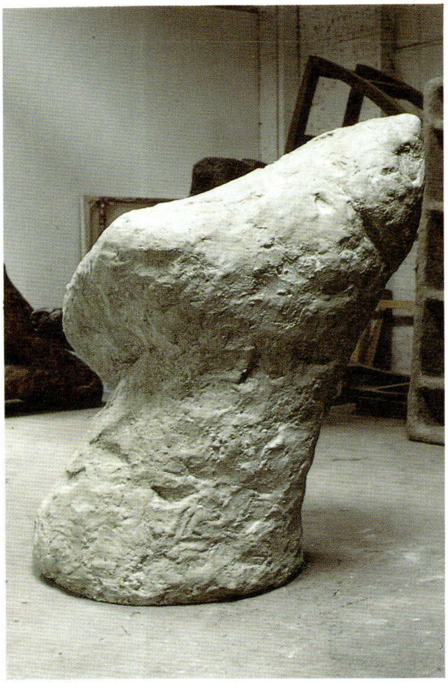

Tethys 1986 (plaster for bronze, cat. no.4)

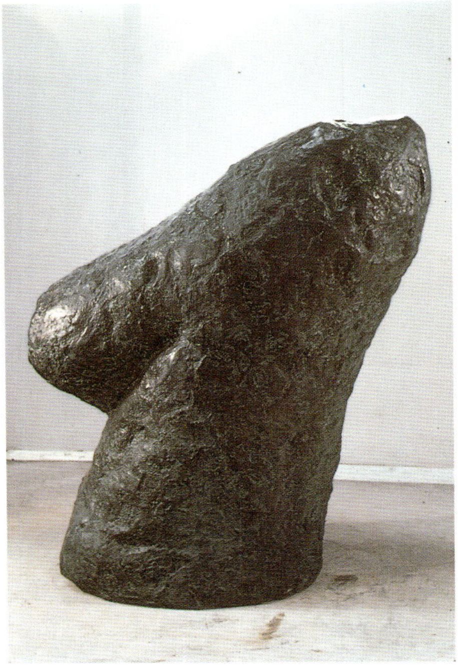

Tethys 1986 (cat.no.4)

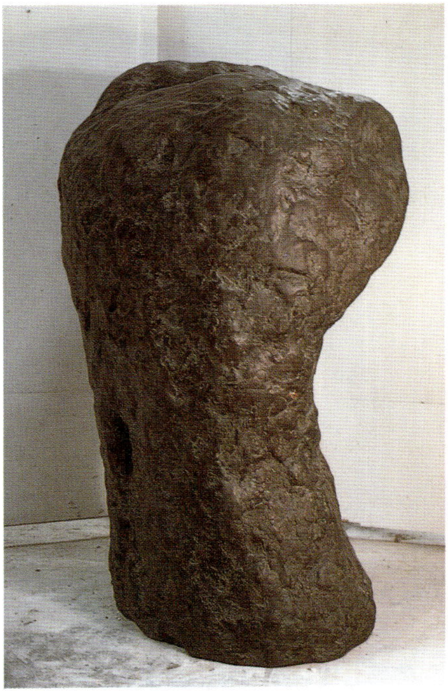

Gaia 1986 (cat.no.5)

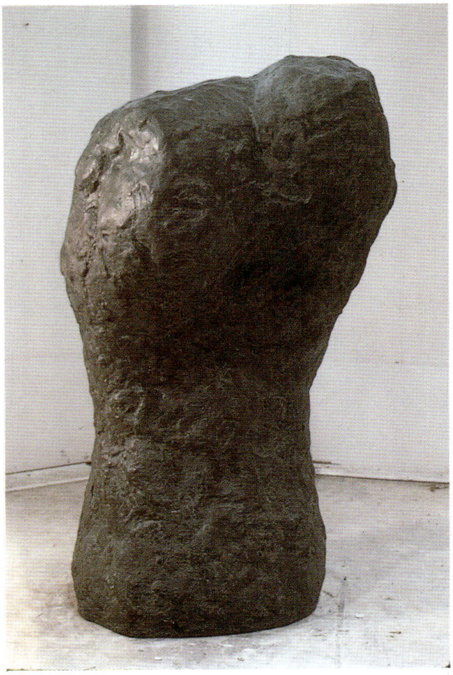

Gaia 1986 (cat.no.5)

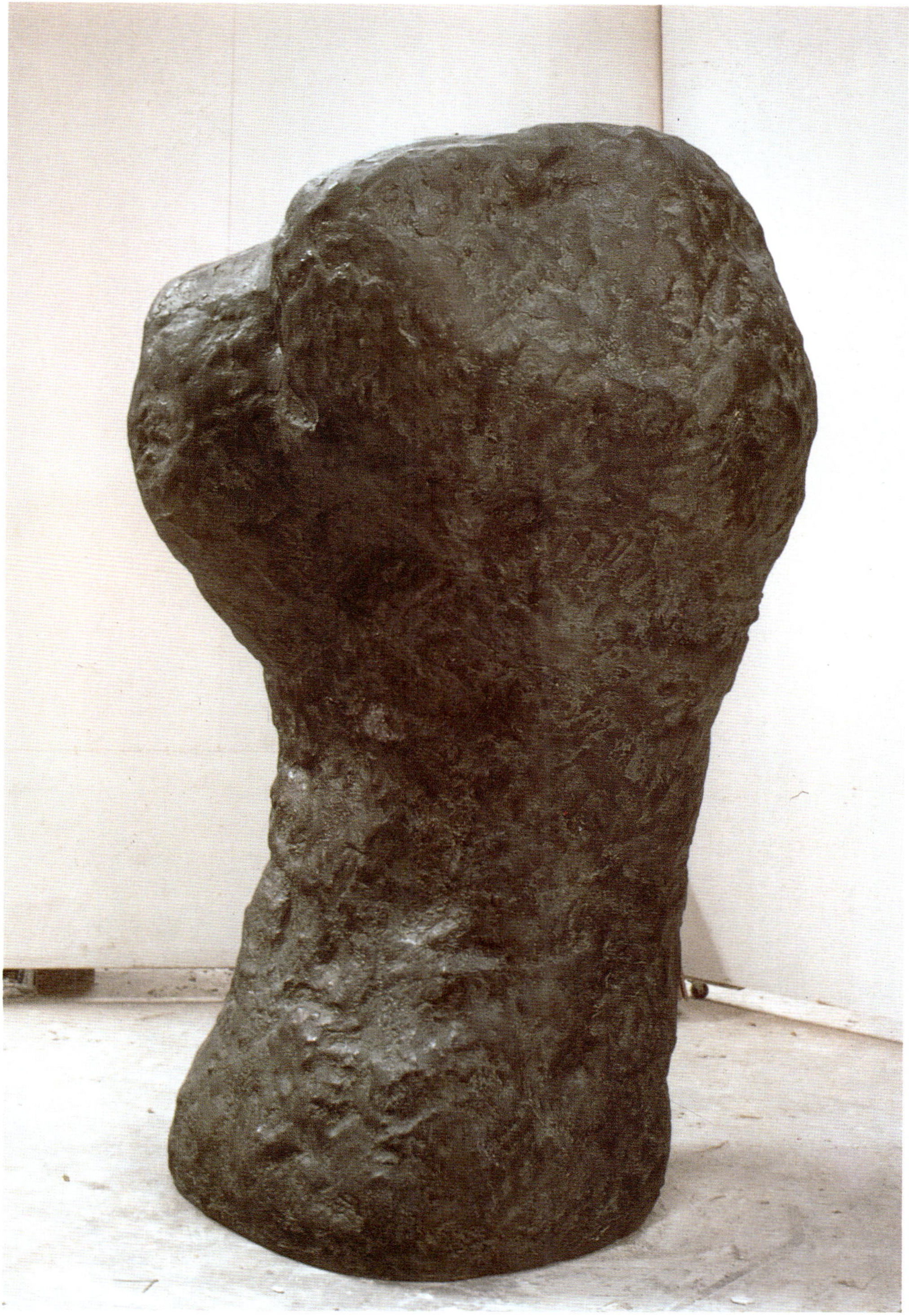

Gaia 1986 (cat.no.5)

Biography

William Tucker was born in Cairo in 1935. His family returned to England in 1937. He studied history at Oxford University (1955-58) and sculpture at Central School of Art and Design and at St Martin's School of Art, London (1959-60). He was awarded the Sainsbury Scholarship, 1961, and the Peter Stuyvesant Foundation Travel Bursary in 1965. He was appointed Gregory Fellow in Sculpture at Leeds University Fine Arts Department (1968-70). In 1974 he published *The Language of Sculpture*. He selected *The Condition of Sculpture* exhibition at the Hayward Gallery and wrote the catalogue essay, 1975. He was Professor of Sculpture at the University of Western Ontario, Canada, 1976. He was taught at St Martin's School of Art (1963-75), Columbia University (1978-82), and the New York Studio School of Painting and Sculpture, 1978-80. In 1981 he was granted a Guggenheim Fellowship for sculpture. In 1977 Tucker moved to the United States and has recently become an American citizen. Tucker lives and works in New York City.

One-Man Exhibitions

1962
Grabowski Gallery, London.
1963
Rowan Gallery, London.
1965
Richard Feigen Gallery, New York.
1966
Rowan Gallery.
1967
Kasmin Gallery, London.
1969
Leslie Waddington Prints, Ltd., London; Leeds City Art Gallery (Gregory Fellow Exhibition); Kasmin Gallery.
1970
Kasmin Gallery.
1972
*British Pavilion, XXXVI Venice Biennale, Italy.
1973
Leslie Waddington; Hamburg Kunstverein, Hamburg, Germany; Museum Bochum, Germany;
*Serpentine Gallery (Arts Council), London.
1976
Wakefield Art Gallery (Drawings); Hester van Royen Gallery, London;
*Galerie Wintersberger, Cologne.
1977
Robert Elkon Gallery, New York.
1978
*Retrospective exhibition, Fruit Market Gallery, Edinburgh, and tour, sponsored by the Arts Council of Great Britain; Sable-Castelli Gallery, Toronto.
1979
Robert Elkon Gallery.
1980
David Reids Gallery, Sydney, Australia; Robert Elkon Gallery; Powell St. Gallery, Melbourne, Australia.
1981
*L'Isola Gallery, Rome.
1982
Bernard Jacobson Gallery, Los Angeles; *Robert Elkon Gallery.
1984
William Tucker - New York, 5 May - 2 June, David McKee Gallery (courtesy of Carla Panicali);
**William Tucker*, Summer 1984, L'Isola Gallery, Rome.
1985
William Tucker - Sculpture and Drawing, 8 February - 13 March, Pamela Auchincloss Gallery, Santa Barbara, California; *William Tucker*, 8-13 May, Chicago International Art Fair '85, Chicago, Ill.; *William Tucker - Three Gymnasts*, 29 June - 26 October, Neuberger Museum, Purchase, New York; *William Tucker - Gymnasts*, 2 November - 14 December, David McKee Gallery (courtesy of Carla Panicali).
1987
William Tucker - Bronzes, 3 March - 1 April, Pamela Auchincloss Gallery, Santa Barbara, California.

Group Exhibitions

1960-61
26 Young Sculptors, Institute of Contemporary Arts, London.
1961
II Biennale de Paris, National Museum of Modern Art, Paris.
1965
New Generation, 1965, Whitechapel Gallery, London; *London, the New Scene*, Walker Art Center, Minneapolis, Minn.
1966
5^{e}Internationale Beeldententoonstellig, Sonsbeek, Holland; *Eight British Sculptors*, Stedelijk Museum, Amsterdam; *Primary Sculpture*, The Jewish Museum, New York.
1967
Sculpture in the Open Air, London County Council, London; Guggenheim International Sculpture Exhibition, The Solomon R. Guggenheim Museum, New York.
1968
Documenta IV, Kassel, West Germany; Orpheus II, 1965 exhibition of British artists, circulated by the Museum of Modern Art, New York International Exhibition of Contemporary Art, Helsinki.
1971
British Painting and Sculpture, 1960-61, National Gallery of Art, Washington, D.C.
1972
British Sculptors, Royal Academy, London.
1975
New Acquisitions - Drawings, The British Museum, London; *Sculpture at Greenwich*, London.

1976
The Biennale of Sydney, Art Gallery of New South Wales, Australia; *Arte Inglese Oggi*, Milan, Italy.

1979
Contemporary Sculpture, Museum of Modern Art, New York; *Prospect Mountain Sculpture Show: *A Homage to David Smith*, Lake George, New York.

1980
Skulptur des 20. Jahrhunderts, Basel, Switzerland; International Sculpture Conference, Washington, D.C.; *Contemporary British Painting and Sculpture*, Museum of Modern Art, Tokyo, Japan; *Drawings by Three Artists*, Betty Cunningham Gallery, New York.

1981
**New Work on Paper*, Museum of Modern Art, New York; *Sculpture by Four: Delap, Hall, Arnoldi, Tucker*, Robert Elkon Gallery, New York; *Recent Editions*, Bernard Jacobson Gallery, Los Angeles; *Il Luogo della Forma*, Museo di Castelvecchio, Verona, Italy; *Bronze*, Patricia Hamilton Gallery, New York; *Group Show*, Diane Brown Gallery, Washington, D.C.

1983
**Monumental Drawings by Sculptors*, Hillwood Art Gallery, C. W. Post Center, Long Island University, Greenvale, NY; *The Sculptural Line*, Damon Brandt Gallery, New York; **Artists Choose Artists II*, CDS Gallery, New York; **The Sculpture Show '83: Selected New Work by 50 Sculptors*, Hayward and Serpentine Galleries, London.

1984
Varieties of Sculptural Ideas, Max Hutchinson Gallery, New York; **Actual Size*, Dalhousie Art Gallery, Halifax, Nova Scotia; **Drawings 1974-1984*, The Hirshhorn Museum and Sculpture Garden, Washington, D.C.; *Seven Sculptors in America*, 1 Penn Plaza, New York, 21 May - September.

1985
**Working in Brooklyn: Sculpture*, 17 October, 1985 - 6 January, 1986, The Brooklyn Museum, Brooklyn, New York; **Transformations in Sculpture: Four Decades of American and European Art*, 22 November, 1985 - 16 February, 1986, The Solomon R. Guggenheim Museum, New York.

1987
The Museum of Modern Art, *Recent Acquisitions*, 25 November, 1986 - 10 February, 1987, New York; The Metropolitan Museum of Art, opening exhibition for The Lila Acheson Wallace Wing, 9 February, 1987.

Public Collections

Aberdeen Art Gallery, Scotland.
Arts Council of Great Britain.
British Council.
British Museum.
Kröller-Müller Museum, Netherlands.
Leicester Education Authority.
Louisiana Museum of Modern Art, Denmark.
Metropolitan Museum, New York.
Museum of Modern Art, New York.
Peter Stuyvesant Foundation.
Storm King Art Center, Mountainville, New York.
Tate Gallery.
The Solomon R. Guggenheim Museum, New York.
University of California at Los Angeles.
Victoria and Albert Museum.
Walker Art Center, Minneapolis.

*Catalogue available

Bibliography

Baro, G., 'Britain's Young Sculptors', *Arts* 40 (December 1965): 14.
Dienst, R. G., 'Drei Aspekte der neuen englischen Plastik', *Kunstwerk* 19 (March 1966): 11-15.
Jouffroy, A., 'Art de demi brume à Londres', *Oeil* 149 (May 1967): 37-38.
Lucie-Smith, E., 'William Tucker and Pol Bury at Kasmin', *Studio* 173 (May 1969): 254.
Ammann, J. C., 'Anthony Caro und die junge englische Skulptur', *Werk* 54 (October 1967): 644.
Kudielka, R., 'London im Herbst', *Kunstwerk* 21 (October 1967): 46.
Melville, R., 'Young Consolidators: The Interim: Show at Whitechapel', *Architectural Review* 144 (July 1968): 64.
Pinney, M., 'Exhibition at Kasmin Gallery', *Arts Canada* 26 (August 1969): 44.
Russell, J., 'New Names in London: A to Z', *Art in America* 58 (September 1970): 99.
Packer, W., 'Kasmin Gallery, London, Exhibition, *Art and Artists* 5 October 1970): 34.
Burr, J., 'London Galleries, Kasmin Art Gallery Exhibition', *Apollo* 92 (November 1970): 385.
Laurens, Henri, 'Exhibition at the Hayward', *Studio* 182 (July 1971): 24-25.
Tucker, William, 'A Note on Rietveld as a Sculptor', *Studio*, April 1972.
Tucker, William, 'Gravity, Rodin, Degas', *Studio*, July 1973.
Martin, Barry, 'Review', *Studio*, July 1973.
Kramer, Hilton, review, *The New York Times,* 21 July 1974; *Art and Artists,* London, May 1975.
Fry, Edward, review, summer 1975, *Artforum.*
Crichton, Fenella, review, *Art International,* June 1975.
Feaver, W., review, *Apollo*, June 1975.
Lucie-Smith, E., review, *Illustrated London News*, June 1975.
Fuller, Peter, review, *New Society*, 5 June 1975.
Alloway, Lawrence, 'Caro's Art - Tucker's Choice', *Artforum* 14 (October 1975): 66-67.
Chapman, Hilary, 'Condition of Sculpture', *Arts* 50 (November 1975): 68-69.
Ashton, Dore, article, *The Art Bulletin*, December 1975.
Elsen, Albert, review of William Tucker's *Early Modern Sculpture, Art Journal* 35 (Winter 1976): 136-178.
Tucker, William 'Road to Tirgu Jiu', *Art in America*, November 1976.
Kramer, Hilton, review, *The New York Times,* 8 April 1977.
Baker, Kenneth, 'William Tucker: Meaning vs. Matter', *Art in America* 65 (November/December 1977): 102-103.
'Modernism, Freedom, Sculpture', *Art Journal,* Winter 1977-78.
Spalding, Frances, 'William Tucker Sculptures (exhibit)', *Connoisseur* 196 (November 1977): 233.
Kramer, Hilton, review, *The New York Times,* 'Triumphant New York by Two Artists', 25 May 1979.
Ashton, Dore, 'William Tucker's Gyre', *Arts* 53 (June 1979): 128-129.
Berlind, Robert, 'Robert Elkon Gallery, New York Exhibit', *Art in America* 67 (October 1979): 122.
'Image as Emblem', *Art in America,* January 1981.
McCorquodale, C., 'William Tucker: Drawings and Sculptures', review, *Arts* 27 (6/27/75).
Shuebrook, Ron, 'William Tucker', *Artscribe* 36 (August 1982), pp.35-43.
Madoff, Steven Henry, 'William Tucker at Robert Elkon Uptown and Downtown', *Art in America,* September 1982, p.163.
Megged, Matti, 'The Sculpture of William Tucker', *Arts* (May-September 1982); 'William Tucker', *Kunstspiegel* 9 (December 1975), for Galerie Wintersberger & Kunst-Borse, Cologne, pp.4-5.
Glueck, Grace, 'Art: Mega to Mini in 2 Shows', *The New York Times,* 24 December 1982.
Russell, John review of 'Artists Choose Artists', *The New York Times,* 6 October 1983; 'Sculpture Elsewhere', *The New York Times,* 8 July 1983.
Forgey, Benjamin, 'The Hirshhorn's Big Draw', *The Washington Post,* 15 March 1984.
Russell, John, 'William Tucker', review; *The New York Times,* 11 May 1985.
Raynor, Vivien, 'Art: Seven Sculptors at Penn Plaza', *The New York Times,* 15 June 1984.
Brenson, Michael, 'A Sculpture Revival All Around Town', *The New York Times.* 1 November 1985.
Russell, John, 'Art: New Sculptures by William Tucker', *The New York Times*, 15 November 1985.
Brenson, Michael, 'Critics' Choices for the Thanksgiving Weekend', *The New York Times,* 29 November 1985.

Publications

The Language of Sculpture, by William Tucker (Thames & Hudson: London, 1974), published in America as *Early Modern Sculpture* (Oxford Univ. Press: 1974).
'The Gonzalez Exhibition', by William Tucker, *The New Criterion*, vol.I, no.9, May 1983.

Note: Carla Panicali is sole agent for William Tucker through her gallery in New York, *Art for Architecture*, and her gallery in Rome, *L'Isola*.

List of Works

1 **Rhea** 1985
Plaster & polyester resin
105 × 63 × 42in (266.7 × 160 × 106.7cm)
The Artist
Courtesy of L'Isola Gallery, Rome

2 **Ouranos** 1985
Plaster & polyester resin
77 × 71 × 59in (195.6 × 180.3 × 149.9cm)
The Artist
Courtesy of L'Isola Gallery, Rome

3 **Kronos** 1985
Bronze
78 × 49 × 42in (198 × 124.5 × 106.7cm)
The Artist
Courtesy of L'Isola Gallery, Rome

4 **Tethys** 1986
Bronze
73 × 61 × 50in (185.4 × 155 × 127cm)
The Artist
Courtesy of L'Isola Gallery, Rome

5 **Gaia** 1986
Bronze
82 × 47 × 43in (208.3 × 119.4 × 322.6cm)
The Artist
Courtesy of L'Isola Gallery, Rome